Presence

Presence

by

Scott Wiggerman

Pecan Grove Press  San Antonio, Texas

Copyright © 2011
by Scott Wiggerman

All rights reserved.

Cover art: "Better Window" by Carol A. King

Copyright © 2011 by Carol A. King
http://www.cKingGalleries.com

Library of Congress Cataloging-in-Publication Data

Wiggerman, Scott.
  Presence / by Scott Wiggerman.
     p. cm.
  ISBN 978-1-931247-95-5
  I. Title.

PS3573.I382P74 2011
811'.54--dc22

2011018055

Pecan Grove Press
Box AL
1 Camino Santa Maria
San Antonio, TX 78228

Acknowledgements

I gratefully acknowledge the following publications, in which these poems first appeared, some in slightly different forms:

Acts of Emancipation (Plymouth Writers Group, 2005): "Release"

Affirming Flame: Writings by Progressive Texas Poets in the Aftermath of September 11th (Evelyn Street Press, 2002): "A Week in the Life," "The Weather Inside"

Austin Chronicle: "Why Mattresses Sag"

Bad News Bingo: "Omnipotence"

Big Tex[t]: "Aboard a Boat on Lake Travis, Memorial Day Weekend"

Borderlands: Texas Poetry Review: "Dogma," "Synecdoche"

BorderSenses: "Chimayo"

A Christmas Collection (July Literary Press, 2001): "Winter Solstice"

Concho River Review: "August"

Connection: Poems Inspired by the Art of Thúy Saliba (2006): "Tracks in the Snow"

di-verse-city: "Transubstantiation," "Power Outage," "Dreams of Fire and Ice"

Divine Animal: "Skin"

Enigmatist: "Two White Moths"

For Better or For Worse (PoetWorks Press, 2005): "Wedding Poem"

Gertrude: "A Matter of Size"

Hiss Quarterly: "Cockfight"

Illya's Honey: "Sound Barrier"

In the Arms of Words: Poems for Disaster Relief (Sherman Asher, 2005): "Surrender"

Möbius: "The Departed" (appeared as "The Disappeared")

Muse Apprentice Guild: "Presence"

New Texas: "Fear of Heights," "On Turning Fifty"

qarrtsiluni: "Baptism"

Other Voices International Project: "Contemplating the Long Grass"

Poetry Depth Quarterly: "Magritte's Perceptions"

Poetry Midwest: "Seven Reasons to Go to Bed with You"

Queer Collection (Fabulist Flash, 2007): "The Interview Date"

San Antonio Express-News: "Vanishing Point"

Sojourn: "Home"

Southwestern American Literature: "Family Wills"

Swell: "Letter to My Father-in-Law"

Texas Poetry Calendar: "The Pecan Trees"

Texas Poetry Journal: "Clarity"

Texas Writer: "All That Remains"

This New Breed: Gents, Bad Boys, & Barbarians 2 (Windstorm Creative, 2003): "Coming Out"

Wild Plum: "Reading Atwood at 30,000 Feet"

Windhover: "The Chosen," "Ways of Leaving"

Contents

Water

Presence	3
The Chosen	4
Seven Reasons to Go to Bed with You	6
A Matter of Size	7
The Will and the Way	8
The Weather Inside	9
Surrender	10
Still January	11
Aboard a Boat on Lake Travis, Memorial Day Weekend	13
The Interview Date	14
Baptism	16

Air

Vanishing Point	21
Reading Atwood at 30,000 Feet	23
Fear of Heights	24
Two White Moths	26
Power Outage	27
The Departed	28
Shoot-Out	29
On Turning Fifty	30
Release	31
Magritte's Perceptions	32

Earth

Chimayo	37
Family Wills	38
Home	41
Why Mattresses Sag	42
Synecdoche	43
Skin	44
Blanca	45
Tracks in the Snow	46
Contemplating the Long Grass	47
Kiss as Manifesto	49
Letter to My Father-in-Law	50

Fire

Sound Barrier	55
Coming Out	56
Dreams of Fire and Ice	60
Winter Solstice	61
Our Place	62
Sun-Drenched Poppies	63
Cockfight	64
Stand-Off	65
A Week in the Life	66
All That Remains	67

Spirit

Omnipotence	71
Wedding Poem	72
Ways of Leaving	73
Dogma	75
Transubstantiation	78
There Is No Saint Named Scott	79
Clarity	80
Berryman's Last Dream Song	81
My Generation	82
Dr. H. Anonymous	83
August	85
The Pecan Trees	86

*for Cathy,
for Margaret,
but especially
for David*

Water

Presence

I am the blood-red stain
on the bone-white cloth
that's been in the family for years.
You can hide me
with a well-placed serving dish
or a garish Texas centerpiece,
but you cannot blot me
from your memory.

You've tried repeated washings,
but my burgundy shadow
continues to disturb.
Strait-laced, God-fearing,
you recite grace around me
and pray I might be cleansed.

As plates are cleared
and conversation spills
to a level furtive as an affair,
I sit quietly, a stigma
that won't stop bleeding.
I can pretend with the best of them,
but the only way to be rid of me
is to throw the tablecloth out.

The Chosen

i.
   As the gray waters rose
   and the sun disappeared for weeks,
   depression descended upon the animals.

   Penguins missed the sparkle of ice,
   monkeys grew claustrophobic without trees,
   groundhogs ached to dig in the earth.

   Ants withdrew without busy colonies,
   owls couldn't tell when to sleep, when to wake,
   Angora goats started losing their hair.

   Wolverines fought like schoolyard children,
   the female beetle thought menopause hit early,
   the male elephant harbored thoughts of suicide.

   Sex, too, proved susceptible to boredom.
   Soon the cobras claimed headaches;
   even the rabbits agreed to separate berths.

   Why, they asked in therapy sessions,
   were we, of all our species, selected to be saved?
   Why were we singled out for this stinking ark?

ii.
    Fish, on the other hand, flourished
    with rain and water everywhere,
    their world an aquarium of new adventures.

    Cod lost their fear of fishermen's nets;
    salmon, their need to run upstream.
    Fish multiplied like loaves of Biblical bread,

    until the lonely dove returned
    with a soggy olive branch,
    proof that the waters were abating.

    When the big boat anchored on Ararat
    with nary a fanfare or cheer—
    depression had shifted to apprehension.

    Kangaroos were alarmed at sinking into the ooze,
    centipedes were unsure of their footing,
    turtles feared to leave their homey shells.

    The weak and weary animals felt
    the terrible burden of procreation
    weigh on them like God's heavy hands.

    Knowing their best was all washed up,
    each creature looked at its mate, warily.
    It was time to learn to love anew.

Seven Reasons to Go to Bed with You

to hear your tongue's waves
push into my shore

      to ride the steady echo
      of your heart's insistent calls

to sail your cloud of skin
as it seeps into my pores

      to mingle with your current
      as you smooth over my edges

to feed a small volcano
with the rumble of your tremors

      to curl like a cave
      swallowed in your arms

to drift into dreams
on the words of your hands

A Matter of Size

This hotel bed is a sea,
a wide swath of quiet
where we float

like distant islands,
almost out of sight.

Waves of white
billow between us;
your breathing

barely reaches my shore.
I long to return home

where we surge,
touch and tumble,
in the brine

of our own small bed.

The Will and the Way

The boys don't swim upstream as well
as they did just years ago. They laze along
while time speeds up, a rush they cannot quell.

Once it took no effort, no need to coax or yell,
for they were fighters, a battle-worthy throng.
Now the boys don't swim upstream that well.

Some nights the blood simply will not jell,
blows now soft that once were hard and strong,
while time speeds up in a rush. You cannot quell

the downhill slide nor raise a hearty swell,
but still you hear desire's call, limpid as a gong.
Why won't the boys swim upstream? Well,

they're gunners out of ammo; orders can't propel
them into service, nor commands prolong
their time, speeding to a rush that none can quell.

Accept decline—that's it in a nutshell—
or fortify the troops. And is it so wrong
that the boys don't swim upstream too well?
For time speeds up, crushes what it cannot quell.

The Weather Inside

Clouds amassed for weeks
where old ones failed to leave,

till gray skies glutted
and light was crushed in their blotter.

With air too black to breathe
and rumbles echoing down streets,

the storm ached deep in his bones.
It felt like a coming heartbreak.

Surrender

She squats in the muck
at the water's edge
as she has for a week,
fixed to the spot
like a lighthouse

sinking.
Her weary eyes stare down
the cinnamon-colored sea,
as if willpower alone
could control its roil,

force it to return
the child she could not
cling to, cannot beacon—
or sweep the urge
from under her feet.

Still January

The cat's been spiraling inward,
her face inseparable from her tail,
a Möbius strip of gray fur.
You've been stratified in sweaters
and sweatshirts, a plush robe
encasing the layers below—
yet you check the thermostat
like a nurse monitors a patient.
At least you move. I haven't
stepped out of the house in two days,
wedged like lost change
among the pillows of the sofa.

Clouds have murked the day
with on-again, off-again drizzle,
the landscape subdued in a trance,
everything wet and forlorn.

All day, I read a novel about 9/11,
glancing out the window
at skies laden in ash,
half-expecting to see bodies
plummet into view,
not seeing so much as a squirrel.
We stay in our homes,
knowing it's no safer here
than anywhere else.

You fidget with your own book,
another cup of green tea,
arms and legs twisted in a huddle
beneath an afghan.
I watch your lips move
with each word
but can't make out a single one.
I think about how the rats in the attic
haven't scratched all weekend.

Aboard a Boat on Lake Travis, Memorial Day Weekend

It all comes down to the ducks.
Each swims aimlessly from slip to slip,
loses the others around bows of boats,
then just as suddenly converges with them
in a mad paddle to stay together.

Taking turns in the captain's seat,
we watch from the upper deck
till they disappear around the end of the pier.
We have bobbed like driftwood for an hour
to the lake's slow but drunken rhythms,
drinking bottled water like we once drank margaritas.

In our passage to get to where we're at,
we've digressed in countless directions,
taken paths as erratic as the ducks'.
I have my poems and the love of a good man.
Cathy has a religion of crystals and labyrinths;
Margaret, at last her house at the lake
and a twin-engined boat of twenty-seven feet.

We watch the waves for ducks, happy,
for we have managed to converge once again.
Next time we may even leave the marina.

The Interview Date

Where are you from?

>What I wanted
>was to watch you speak,
>see the pink raft of tongue
>lap at your lips,
>the beacon of Adam's apple,
>beckon up and down.

How long have you lived here?

>What I wanted
>was to watch you lean in,
>observe the swells of hair
>eddying from your shirt,
>the surge of nipples,
>hard as a rocky coast.

Where did you go to school?

>What I wanted
>was to watch you stand,
>gauge the strain of your anchor,
>note the cove of buttocks,
>lean as the Strait of Gibraltar,
>a tight figure-eight.

What do you do for fun?

    What I wanted
    was to leave the coffeeshop,
    shuck you like an oyster,
    raise your mast,
    unfurl your sails,
    ride you into the night—

    but that would wait
    till the second date.

Baptism

A young man stares into the sun,
seizes air through his mouth
like one who's been under water too long,
lungs filling with the deep scents
of mud and summer grasses.

He steps out of his sandals,
strips off his shirt and shorts,
and slips into the shallow creek,
hips wedged on the rocky bottom,
body prone as a makeshift raft.

Cold water bristles over and under
his limbs; his pale torso
bobs like a thin pink float.
The eyes of the world retreat
as hate sloughs away like dead skin.

All that is left is blue sky,
warm sun, cool water,
and a rhythmic trickle
that matches beat for beat
the drumming of a buoyant heart.

Air

Vanishing Point

I perfected risotto that summer,
but suspect I began to fade
long before that,
evaporating like broth
into pale, white essence.

Did I begin to wane
as early as December,
a crisp night at opposite ends
of a sweltering hot tub,
heat bubbling from the surface,
my face dissipating
in the steam?

Or was it spring
when I began to taper away?
On a bicycle ride, possibly,
down a country road in Texas,
my figure shrinking
as I rode ahead and became
a problem of perspective:
the smaller I got,
the more I looked like him.

I will never know at what point
I started to disappear,
to filter away like hourglass sand,
but, grain by grain,

I lost substance
till I vanished completely
from your world.

Reading Atwood at 30,000 Feet

Azure expanses offer no clarity,
only more distance.
I could just as well be over Canada,
Siberia, someplace cold,
as over the American Southwest.
From here, everything is remote:
cities, oceans, failure.

My spine in an upright position,
I removed myself from attendants' orders
and the hiss of artificial air
even before takeoff.
Strapped in an aisle seat,
I rigidly continue to read.

A glance out the window reveals
what is to be expected
when the world as we know it
has been relinquished:
emptiness, nothing.

I take no comfort in knowing
that seats can be used as flotation devices,
as if any body of water
exists between Austin and Albuquerque.

But I do dream of surfacing,
rising out of a ghostly lake;
of gulping air, pungent and pure,
and shimmering like light on water.

Fear of Heights

It starts with a jolt, a raw metallic creak,
before it lurches upward in a labor of physics.

The cables, overgrown clotheslines, don't look
like they could handle a load of forty tourists,

yet in the crush of a cabin surrounded by glass,
we slowly ascend on the tram's giant pulley.

Despite the twilight, I can still make out
the brown-red granite of boulders below,

the stern veneer of weathered cliffs,
spires and pinnacles eroding above the canyon,

their size put into perspective only by pine trees,
enormous, but dwarfed by the mass of the Sandias.

In the pit of my stomach, something contracts,
and my grip instinctively tightens on the rail.

Years earlier, panic ensued when I was suspended
at the top of a Ferris wheel (no seatbelts then),

legs dangling in the air like a marionette,
ears attuned to each axle's every squeal,

a single bar of metal all that held me from freefall.
I hover far higher above the ground now,

but I trust in ways that I could not then.
I shut my eyes, inhale the naked mountain air,

let it channel deeply throughout my body;
then I open them to the ethereal sight

of a desert floor coming alive with light,
my hands grasping for nothing.

Two White Moths

A single blue star quivers
at an acute distance.

Two white moths batter
the bleak patio light.

I shut the blinds and retire
to a blanketless bed.

Words like tiny caskets lie
on the nightstand, reminders

of what's been started
and what's not finished,

ink already fading
into an obscure universe.

Would faith be less desolate
if the heavens were attainable,

if those moths
could beat the light?

Power Outage

When a house stops breathing,
familiar sounds vanish:
the air conditioner's hum,
ceiling fans' rattle and swish,
refrigerator's steady drone—
motors and currents replaced
by rumbles of distant thunder
and a percolation of raindrops
through oaks and pecans.

For the first time in months,
we open wide the windows,
allow the storm's fresh breath
to resuscitate our home.

But for sporadic flashes of lightning,
the world outside is black.
We gaze through the serendipitous flicker
of candles too long unlit.
Our fingers meld together.
The dark is quietly comforting;
the slow and simple evening, inviting.

The Departed

I have orphaned many a pair of socks.
Half a dresser drawer is piled
with the carcasses of their mates.
If only it stopped with a stray argyle.

A pair of pants vanished;
a turquoise ring was suddenly gone.
Soon spoons were missing,
slats from mini-blinds, light bulbs,
a fan blade, a framed photograph
and its hook.

I picture a two-room apartment,
perhaps in Peoria or Kokomo,
its tattered walls lined with the missing
ephemera of my life—
all those t-shirts, all those forks,
all those white, beige, brown, and black socks,
forlorn, alone, alive.

Shoot-Out

A deadly black bullet,
one grackle shoots into the yard,
ricocheting from deck to bench
and back again. Another,
on the edge of the gutter,
sits as quiet as a decoy
watching the busy bird below.
Their eyes fix on each other,
stare each other down
like gunfighters of the Old West.

I've seen that look lately,
the impending death-stare,
the glint of steel in your eyes,
unspoken words thick as
black smoke in the air,

and I wonder which of us
will be the first to leave.

On Turning Fifty

No longer able to see them,
we talk around our range of dreams.
They float like clouds, we suspect,
among the peaks, up there somewhere,
like that legendary guru divining wisdom.

We long ago surrendered the means
to climb such lofty pinnacles,
ropes and harnesses tossed in the trash
or sold for pennies at garage sales.
Leave scaling mountains to the young,
who continue to believe they'll be rock stars
or write the Great American novel.
They can fall from great heights—
and still get up. We sympathize,
yet have to laugh at their folly.

While they look up, we look straight ahead,
or down, grounded by bifocals and arthritis.
Dreams are too distant, abstract as math,
so we focus on what we see before us:
no *could be's* or *could have been's*,
no switchbacks or regrets.

As we start the inevitable downward slope,
our paths have never been clearer.
Let others talk into the face of mountains.

Release

She hears gargled whispers,
not the *ahs* of an open throat:
something's caught there.

She hears it again,
ka-ka-ka-ka,
a small bird lodged in the larynx:
cancer.

She curls in a nest,
not a womb,
but a briar of fear.

Hidden within the sinew,
among the muscle's twigs and branches,
in the bone's gray shadows,

a snake closes about her,
its thick black rope
twisting, severing.

She rasps for release,
for the *ah, ah, ah* of life,
but gurgles the word *amen*.

Magritte's Perceptions

A rock is not a rock,
a cloud is not a cloud.
Day could be night,
or night might be day.

An easel sits in front of a window,
but you cannot tell where the canvas ends
or where the landscape takes over;
whether the window looks onto a field
or whether either exists at all.
The juxtaposition is seamless.

The sun is a hole in a tree.
The tree is an opening in a sky.
A face is hidden by a green apple,
a white bird suspended in flight.
But does the apple fall?
Do the wings of the dove ever flutter?

The pipe is not a pipe.
The artist makes that clear:
Ceci n'est pas une pipe.
But if it is not a pipe,
is it then an illusion?

Perhaps the mysterious man
in the bowler and overcoat knows,
the man who looks like
every other man.

Nothing is as it seems.

Earth

Chimayo

I ate dirt yesterday.
Cathy would be proud.

The *santuario* has stood
for almost two hundred years.
Who knows over that time
how many have made the pilgrimage
to taste of its healing dirt?

If you stop at the wood-carved altar,
fail to wander through two low side-doors,
you might miss the discarded crutches,
the hole in the floor, the dirt,
the scoop perched in it.

I sifted and pinched the dirt
between my fingers,
dropped it in my mouth
like chewing tobacco.
Cathy would have taken a handful,
but she's a walker of holy pilgrimages,
a believer.

All I know is that I still
have that pain in my side,
and even after brushing,
I'm biting down on grit
between my teeth.

Family Wills

i.
On several occasions I shook his hand,
with its two missing fingers, like grasping a claw.

But these times were few—perhaps once a year,
when your sons are in Texas

and you arrange for them to see their grandfather—
never as public as weddings or funerals

or other extended family gatherings
where I am neither invited nor allowed.

We meet halfway in neutral San Antonio,
at a Mexican restaurant where your father knows

the owners, like his father did before him:
Jacala's is rigged with history against me.

We always arrive late, which gives him time
to liquor up on tequila, only the premium kind.

The seating has been arranged in advance:
grandfather and grandsons at one end of the table,

you and your brothers buffered in the middle,
your sister and me at the other end.

Depression descends like a black mantilla,
and I bide time through each drawn-out joke

(which I swear are the same ones
he stupefied us with at last summer's meal).

Everyone laughs because everyone knows
exactly what the old man expects—

but he never expected a gay son who would leave
a wife and two children, and he never expected me.

He has never stepped foot in our house;
after I answered the phone one time,

he also stopped the occasional call.
Years later, "Hi, how are you?" is still an effort.

He looks directly through me
like I'm an empty seat at the end of the table.

The Tex-Mex platter, dun-colored and greasy,
is a reminder I should have stayed home.

ii.
I've only seen photographs of the farm
where he lost his fingers in an accident,

machinery fallow and rusting near the barn.
This time I *am* home, sick for a week and pissed

that you've driven three and a half hours
to attend the annual Christmas gathering,

that you've chosen them over me.
I find out later that a cousin asked about me,

but the rest of the family went on pretending
you are straight and single. Or do they

still think of you as married? You should
have been back by now, so I brood,

your death looming like a bright red poppy.
Cruel as your father, I decide your ashes

will be scattered in a Hill Country field
before I ever let him know what's happened.

Home

He posits fiber and fur,
acorn-colored sheaves of bark,
feathers retrieved from crooks of trees,
shoots and tendrils, tawny filaments.

He glues together bits of shell
with albumen and tempera's yolk,
constructs an egg-shaped hull,
a mosaic of porous fragments.

Ecru walls rise about him
like petals closing for the night.
He seals the last piece in place.
Almost translucent, his fragile cocoon
is warm, not dark; safe, not lonely.

Why Mattresses Sag

In the heart of the night
bodies drift to the heart of the bed

as though they are magnets
and the center is true north.

Torsos cook against each other
like sweat lodge rocks,

sizzling in a jumble of limbs
and scents and flesh and fur,

needs that speak an unfiltered language,
a love song, a sigh, a release

before the breach of daylight.

Synecdoche

—inspired by Byron Kim's painting "Synecdoche"

Skin is a layer that's ever so slight,
a bounty of pigment, sometimes a dearth,
though never pitch black and never pure white.

Some skin recedes like the sun into night,
its coral horizon pink as a birth,
lit like falling stars, but ever so slight.

Some skin is almost an absence of light,
a deeply dug soil the umbers of earth,
but never pitch black. Nor ever pure white,

but flushed as a flock of cardinals in flight,
or beige as a beach, ashen as a hearth,
the skin's a coating that's ever so slight.

And would we sense if we did not have sight
the differing shades that drive a wide berth
on a scale between pitch black and pure white?

Beneath our façades, where colors unite
in muscle and tissue equal in worth,
skin's just a veneer that's ever so slight.
It's never pitch black and never pure white.

Skin

Then there's a lover's skin,
the tentative touch of fingers on flesh
like a bomb squad approaching
a mysterious package,
a combination of caution and commotion
ready to explode at your fingertips.

There's the rush to unearth his geography,
contour the soft plains and rough terrains,
rolling muscles and nervous valleys;
explore his equators, map his jungles,
detect and record his imperfections—
the twin joys of uncovering and discovering.

And there's the tingle that comes,
the shiver of goose bumps
charged as electric particles
stimulated by your own reactor,
flesh alert as a watchdog,
ready to growl or yowl
like the moon tickling the horizon.

Blanca

Moored to limbs as brown as dust,
the sycamore's leaves haven't whispered
this February, but clattered and groused
like wind-up teeth, mocking and unjust.
The pecans' have long since disappeared,
arms bare and silent, like the empty house
all week. Each sudden glimpse of white—
sunlight patterned on the carpet, underwear
left on the bed—has made me cleave
to shadows, to realize again how finite
and temporal are the years. In the lair
of the gray tree with clattering leaves:
the tamped mound of dirt, the soft fur,
a sound more like a pigeon, your purr.

Tracks in the Snow

You, of course, see red.
The barn could be the size
of a dollhouse, but as long
as it is red, the barn
is what you'll remember.
I am drawn to black and white.
It's how I see the world.
I follow black tracks
carved into white snow
to a gray fence that delineates
one white field from another,
shadowy earth to shadowy sky.
The red barn is an unwanted
guest in my landscape.
I have only to lift my hand
to reduce it to a black roof
buried under a white veil.
If you force me, I can do
the same with you.

Contemplating the Long Grass

The sky is as gray
as the bottom of my bathtub,

which reminds me,
it's been a month since I cleaned

and dustballs in the hall
dance when I walk by,

follow me into the living
room, which reminds me

that I never got around
to reading the stack

of magazines on the coffee table,
and now I'm three months

behind on *Cooking Light*,
which reminds me,

I never did make
the Thai recipe for

grilled beef salad
that I clipped from the paper,

though I did buy
lemongrass for the dressing,

which reminds me that I
also bought figs that day,

so I look in the bin
of the refrigerator, and sure

enough, there's a mushy mass,
gray as the impending sky,

so I guess I won't mow
after all.

Kiss as Manifesto
—based on Constantin Brancusi's sculpture "The Kiss"

Some don't see it,
such as my father-in-law.
But the two are one,
sheltered in a limestone kiss,
an embrace as constant
as a circle.

Because they are one,
their sex unchiseled,
differences are not discernable.
They could be two women.
They could be two men.

Eye to stony eye,
they exist for each other.
Boxed into a world
some don't want to see,
the two are solid, inseparable,
one.

Letter to My Father-in-Law

I rode your son real hard last night,
broke him like a wild stallion,
head pulled back, nostrils wide as moons,
feral cries piercing midnight's marrow.
Both of us panting at breakneck speed,
the rank sweat of man transformed to beast,
effusive as a newly drilled oil well.
You must know about cowboys and oil.

I believe it will happen someday, even in Texas,
the day when marriage between men is legal.
I will spare you the embarrassment of attending.
You won't be invited, won't have to worry
about witnessing our kiss before God's good altar.
You will be as welcome at my wedding as I was at yours.
Think of it, old man, as my gift to you.

I thought that once you met me I would become
something more than the Yankee faggot
that you *think* led your son astray.
True, I didn't wear boots or a five-inch buckle,
but I left the boa and eye-liner at home.
I walked and talked as straight as a ruler,
though I may as well have bent over.

I'm reconciled to the fact that you'll be dead
before I ever set foot on your farm.
I should like to see the house your son grew up in,

the acres he worked, the home he escaped.
But the biggest draw will be standing on the land
that I'd been banned from, knowing that you
will be in your grave, writhing without a shotgun,
when your son and I get down in your dirt.

Fire

Sound Barrier

This silence is shattered.
Tiny shards of quiet
embed in my feet
so that with each step
I remember the pain
of where I've been.

I cannot speak
in complacent tongues
or conspire with those
who prefer I were mute.

My feet have hardened,
lost the path of least resistance,
adapted like young amputees.
I am prepared to walk across coals
and listen to the crackle of molten glass.

Coming Out

i. *Denial*

Denial is the overprotective parent,
the stubborn disciplinarian,
the nun's unrelenting stare.
It is the insidious root
that stunts desires, reins in dreams,
buries your head in the sand.

Denial leads you on a leash,
has you sniff in the dirt for scraps,
tail tightly glued
to the taboo between your legs.

Denial lines your head
like a papier-mâché pulp
hardened with sentiments
from corrupted fortune cookies:
"It cannot, must not, be."
"It cannot, must not, be me."

ii. *Anger*

He speaks, and blood spits
from his black tongue,
a blistering venom
to lash at a world
that taints him queer.

Shards of glass
grind through his veins,
course behind eyes
that slice like broken mirrors.

He would breathe the fire
of an embittered dragon,
but there are swords
lodged deep in his throat.

He chokes on a hate
so obsidian it could crush bone,
so rancid it could turn love into piss.

iii. *Bargaining*

He loves his wife and three children;
he doesn't want to hurt or lose them.

So he peruses the "alternative" personals,
but never allows himself to call them.
He seeks gay chat rooms on the net,
but always logs on anonymously.
He purchases pornography by mail,
but hides it in a locked desk drawer.

And when he's sufficiently aroused,
he goes to bed with his patient wife,
pecks her cheek like she's his heart's desire.

Then, steeped in sweat, he falls asleep
and dreams about fucking a man.

iv. *Depression*

To find yourself you must lose yourself.
You have to think about loss.

Friends who will suddenly fear
to have you hold their children.

Brothers who won't shake hands,
though you used to share a bath.

Parents who prefer to pretend
that their son no longer exists.

Employers who won't hire you,
or will find an excuse to fire you.

Doctors who won't see you
and feel you deserve no cure.

Religions that hate the sin
but claim to love the sinner.

Governments that don't ask
and will not let you tell.

You have to think about loss,
as a beginning and not an end.

v. *Acceptance*

I have passed for straight,
but not without the shame
of denial dirtying my skin.

I have swallowed anger by the fistful,
conspired with hate,
and stuffed my mouth with silence.

I have bargained with lies,
cowered in closets,
hidden in clothes that never fit right.

I have buried myself
in a suicidal footnote,
when grieving for justice
left me hopeless as stone.

I have lived this poem
for enough of a lifetime—
but no more.

I've come too far
to ever go back.

Dreams of Fire and Ice

You look so masculine with your hands
in flames, eager to destroy or enlighten,
veins and motives hidden in the blaze.

I lie fractured and distressed, a block
of ice paralyzed with the anxiety
that my cold exterior is not an act.

You approach, red-hot energy flickering
up your spine, a leaf of fire blazing over
your head as though touched by spirit.

I withdraw, withhold, a frigid cube
of shame and desire, afraid that I
won't melt, just as afraid I will.

Winter Solstice

When sun stands still,
they light their candles,
place them in cold windows.

The whole world leans
on this deeply curtailed day,
while light is scarce and failing.

Yet holly prospers,
green with the glow
of the new year's promise.

And magic occurs,
as incandescent flames
leap from windows to souls.

Our Place

We slip from our skins,
no longer tethered to blood and bone,
no longer apart, but part of

water in restless currents,
particles billowing in sunlight,
granules, impossible to define,

speaking in leaf and grass,
listening through rock and sand,
touching as wholly as air on air,

one tongue, one ear, effortless,
the world in us unleashed.
Loss is not the return

to telephones and groceries—
it's failure to retain a taste of fire,
this uncomplicated flicker, our place.

Sun-Drenched Poppies

Wait till they are
fully open, like hands
offering peace.
Snip the stems the length
of a simple gift.
Employ them
to dip the flowers
into a fondue of sun.
Hold them there
to the count of blessings.
Lift the dripping poppies
from the cauldron
as if witnessing
a resurrection.
Rejoice at the flare-up
of vibrant reds and oranges.
Pray you'll remember
this luminous dazzle.

Cockfight

Each circles the other,
swollen, swooning,
charged with danger
and desire.

Flaunting, flirting,
each spars a tango,
ruffles plumage,
sizes the other up.

Their red heads brush,
dance apart hastily,
veins engorged
like fuel lines.

Their only eye,
hell-bent, sweating,
rivets to its target,
steels for the long haul.

Stand-Off

We went to bed like boars, but now
we wake without the strength to fight.
How we lose our passions, and how
the day shades with echoes of night.

Still we brood from hostile corners,
hold on to thoughts of wrong or right
like burnished martyrs, lost mourners—
the day shades with echoes of night.

Lights are dimmed. Love is kept in tow.
We, as polar as black and white,
speak with silence, watch the hours go.
The day shades with echoes of night.

A Week in the Life

By the third day,
I could finally read a paper
without drenching the newsprint,
watch the evening news
for fifteen minutes at a time
before succumbing to statistics
of bodies and their parts.

By the fourth day,
I could at last reach out,
but not without seeing
flames in your eyes,
not without tasting
thick gray ash on your lips.

By the fifth day,
I could immerse myself in images:
firemen with Social Security numbers
painted on their arms and legs,
New Yorkers lined up like Argentinians
with photos of their own *desaparecidos.*

By the sixth day,
I could feel the numbness return,
less afraid of a terrorist's attack
than of the blind plunge
into war with an invisible enemy.

All That Remains

The stars are scars on the skin of night:
with inky fold of thickening crust,
a body of black, pinpricked by light.

Fingers like fossils twist in a fright.
Mirrors reveal a pavilion of disgust,
where stars are scars on the skin of night.

Knees give out; the frame grows slight.
Eyes haze over, burn, then combust
to bodies of black, pinpricks of light.

The memory wavers, then loses the fight,
for all must shuffle from dust to dust.
The stars are scars on the skin of night.

Energy dwindles, as does the appetite.
Souls extinguish until they are just
bodies of black, pinpricked by light.

The past is shrunken, the present is trite;
to the future remains a glimmer of trust.
The stars are scars on the skin of night,
a body of black, pinpricked by light.

Spirit

Omnipotence

Seedlings, tiny green planets
drawn like compass points
in the same diurnal direction,
imperfectly lined up
in an ordered microcosm.

In this universe, I am god,
master planner, wielder of life—
all the terrible responsibilities
a higher power should possess.

If the seedlings don't flourish,
bear fruit, or grow straight,
should I withhold their water,
yank them out like some vile weed,
burn them, hate them, ignore them?

Not an angry,
but a benevolent being,
I love the hopeful lives,
tiny necks outstretched,
green tongues shimmering
toward the sun.

Wedding Poem

Suppose Plato was right:
that we are only half a whole,
a left shoe useless without a right,
a negative stammering through life
in search of its elusive positive.

Suppose our search is innate,
a desire so strong, so primitive,
that without that other half
we ache from constant hunger.
No matter how satisfied our appetites,
we seem always to starve for more.

Suppose we find that other half
and slide hard into love's spell,
our unfulfilled yearning as intense
as our need to eat or breathe.
As mysterious as levitation,
our lives are bound together,
though we never know exactly why.

Suppose Plato was right,
that love is the pursuit of the whole,
the fulfillment of an ancient need,
two halves becoming one soul,
melding one into the other,
the end of endless questioning,
the beginning of true union.

Ways of Leaving

I draw into myself like one of the aged,
quiet as the withered sticks huddled in wheelchairs.
Do they hear the rasp of death, smell the nettle of urine,
or are these things reserved for those whose senses
have not yet dribbled to numbness?

We're led down a hall to your grandmother's "suite,"
partitioned with a sheet like an emergency room.
We pass her roommate, a weathered reed
propped in front of a fuzzy television screen.
You introduce me to Granny, and I gingerly
shake her hand, afraid that it might snap.
You told me it took three grown men to pry her
from her home, something I find hard to believe.

From the aisle, I watch you talk with Granny,
as her ninety-seven years beseechingly reach out.
No one in my family ever gets this old.
Her slurred words drool like reluctant tears,
even after she removes her ill-fitting teeth.
Her body, a precarious branch, teeters toward the headboard.
You reposition her, secure her with a strong arm,
kiss without thought the spoiled peach of her cheek.

I try not to touch anything in this place,
even the armchair, as if old age were contagious.
I take in the remnants of a life outside—
photographs, cards, pictures of saints,
a calendar a month out of date—
carelessly taped to institutional walls,
as if anything else would be too permanent.
I settle my gaze on a window that cannot be opened.

As we leave, I wonder how many have died
in the long, long hour we've been here,
how long it takes the living to notice.
I want my death to be quick, if not easy;
for the first time in years, I pray.

Dogma

In a school of Marys and Stevens,
Gregorys and Margarets—
everyone named after saints, popes,
or much-touted martyrs—
I stuck out like a Muslim,
the only one without a patron saint.
Even then I suspected it was a sign.

Perhaps it was early defiance
that kept me from being an altar boy.
When the Johns and Michaels
busied themselves in surplices
at the front of the church,
I sat in a pew, waiting for a calling,
with the Lauras and Rachels. None of us
would ever touch a sepulcher.

Friday mornings, we left our thermoses
and tuna sandwiches on our desks,
made a pilgrimage to that mysterious black box
imbued with incense and sweat, the confessional.
I waited my turn with the Davids and Dianes,
their fingers wrapped around rosaries.
The tips of my fingers were
bloodied from nail-biting,
as if I had sins as thick as bark to unburden.
Every week it was the same thing,
whether or not I had anything to confess:

I disobeyed my parents,
I missed Mass, etc.
I rejoined the other penitents,
dressed alike in gray and navy blue,
and folded my hands in the steeple position.

Friends' homes were rife
with crosses, relics, and holy water,
fronds of palms that had been blessed;
the only thing religious in my house,
buried in the hi-fi, was a family Bible,
kept solely for records and tradition.
I secretly gloated, for when the Communists came—
as we'd been assured by nuns they would—
I knew I would be spared,
for my home had no proof of Christianity.
I knew I would deny and renounce,
life more important than faith.

I excelled at Confirmation for I could
memorize pools of appropriate responses,
phrases as sterile as an operating room.
The Catherines and Raymonds
were filled with renewed spirit,
clutching like parachute cords
their scapulars and medals of St. Christopher.
I never wore anything around my neck.

In church I gazed at stained glass,
more interested in luminescent colors
than anything the priest had to say,
even when the Latin switched over to English.
I fainted one day during Mass.
Several parishioners carried me out.
Gasping for air, I awoke to rays of sunlight.
This was my moment of rapture,
the sign that I'd been seeking—
space, air, a God of skies and clarity;
my body outside the doors of Catholicism
as my mind had always been.

Transubstantiation

Rags cover the flesh
of the bone-house,
a place where soul
has yet to be found
among kidneys or heart.

They say God's words
taste like mead or manna,
but my tongue's known
blood and semen,
a tinge of excrement.

I don't seek salvation
or harbor regrets
for a sudden hereafter.
Flesh is enough;
its dust becomes my host.

There Is No Saint Named Scott

I try to practice patience. Sainthood comes
uneasily. I want to get all Zen,
a lotus, index fingers grazing thumbs,

a mantra on my lips. The pall of ten
returns instead, assigned to work in groups—
to wait on those less able, grip my pen

so tight the Bic becomes a weapon. *Whoops*,
I'd think, its shaft ajar in someone's neck,
I should have worked alone—no nincompoops,

dear teach. I'd earned the brand of smart-aleck
who wouldn't play with others. Now, I try
to be more tolerant on my great trek

toward convert oozing cool. And yet the lie:
my patience darkens Dharma's inner eye.

Clarity

It's never clear. When one is certain of
the real thing, a casual wind will blow
the shifting borders of the land of love,

shuffle the hills of the universe, whereof
a sand dune stares you in the face—though
it's never clear when. One is certain of

death, it's true. You're hit from above
by a lightning bolt—and it's over, bro.
The shifting borders of the land of love

move like tides, encroaching in unheard of
ways—they creep, they leap, they grow—
it's never clear when. One is certain of

taxes, a nun's glare, a subway shove,
but cast doubts on the heart's undertow,
the shifting borders of the land of love.

Just when you think it fits like a glove,
a sinkhole collapses, a valley fills—ergo,
it's never clear! When one is certain of

a love that lasts, a mate as faithful as a dove,
you find yourself with nothing to show.
It's *never* clear when one is certain of
the shifting borders of the land of love.

Berryman's Last Dream Song

Brusque Henry huffed briskly onward
as though late for an important appointment.
Below the Washington Bridge, the frozen
Mississippi beckoned like a bottomless bar drink,
Henry's demons everywhere.
Time to clean things up, he said.

Henry hauled himself onto the rail,
sat and listened to the chime of the bells
from the University—nine times,
a countdown to blast-off. The flesh
of the palms, the seat of the pants, stuck
to the icy rails, not quite ready to give up.

The drop was swift, like that fateful bullet,
his father's maddening legacy.
Some thought he was waving goodbye,
but Henry, his white beard parting like a soul
from its body, was greeting Mr. Bones
and all those acquaintances, pale and old.

My Generation

We knew not what we had to prove each night,
laid back in raw tumescent reveries
when fate could take us anywhere. The fight
was there, the drive to make a mark, to seize
the world and grab it by the balls—at least
it started out that way. The world fought back,
attacked and maimed illusions. Dreams decreased,
ambitions took a hit, and hopes turned black
as oil. We lost too much: the need to prove
ourselves, the chance for better lives, the quest
for health and joy and peace, the whole damned groove
of hippied youth. We failed the acid test.
A parody for generations, we
have shown the jaded world how not to be.

Dr. H. Anonymous
—for Dr. John Fryer, the man behind the mask

The *H.* could stand for harried,
haunted, hunted,
but my intent was homosexual,
a humble attempt at humor.

In fact, *H.* could just as well be hang-up.
Why else would I have appeared
in a parody of drag
with that ridiculous mask and wig?

Not convinced the disguise alone
would be sufficient to hide my identity,
I kept a decoder at the microphone—
that's how deep my horror ran

that you, my honorable peers,
my fellow psychiatrists,
would ferret me out.
I was as closeted as the next gay in 1973,

as worried about losing my career,
but I knew we did not have a "mental disorder,"
that we had no place in the *DSM*,
our Hallowed bible of mental health.

The need to address this wrong
weighed on me like decades of guilt,
and when no one else came forward,
I agreed to take a chance—

under the cloak of anonymity.
I almost backed out when I saw you,
an overflow convention crowd,
but I'd come this far,

and I knew there had to be some supporters—
hell, I'd slept with some of you!
I never expected my small speech
to lead to anything big,

much less a vote that would produce
the happiest headline of my life:
Twenty Million Homosexuals Gain Instant Cure!
I never expected *H.* to stand for hero.

August

Rain barrels are empty,
a sludge of bugs and muck,
dried up like the gutters,
the deck, the grass, the heart.

Nests of bagworms hang
from trees like dirty clouds;
the usual clamor of cicadas
diminished to waves of echoes.
Roaches slink indoors, but
they too lack the spirit to react,
not even scurrying, easily whacked.

You don't have to be told
about drought to know thirst:
everything thirsts.

I venture into the backyard
only long enough to shift the hose,
keep things alive
another day, perhaps a week.
How to keep the heart going
when it's packed down like adobe,
so hard, water runs right off it?

The Pecan Trees

The last leaves have given up,
limbs laid bare as driftwood,
the gray of winter creeks.

The yard is littered with small branches,
broken fingers, crooked, cracked.
I never see them fall—never!—

but there they are, strewn
across the ashen grass,
the debris of abandoned resolutions.

Bent low to the earth,
I gather and clear them—
leaves, twigs, all the dead things

that have collected around me—
testaments to December's end,
the prayers of another year.

2010-2011 Books from Pecan Grove Press

Ahl, Liz. *Luck.* 2010.
ISBN: 978-1-931247-75-7 $7

Ayres, Lana Hechtman. *A New Red.* 2010.
978-1-931247-82-5 $15

Aitches, Marian. *Ours Is a Flower.* 2010.
ISBN: 978-1-931247-78-8 $15

Balcárcel, Rebecca. *Palabras in Each Fist.* 2010.
ISBN: 978-931247-60-6 $15

Byrne, Edward, ed. *Poetry from Paradise Valley.* 2010.
ISBN: 978-1-931247-86-3 $15

Case, Susana H. *The Cost of Heat.* 2010.
ISBN: 978-1-931247-81-8 $7

Greene, Jeffrey. *Beautiful Monsters.* 2010.
ISBN: 978-1-931247-77-1 $15

Haddad, Marian. *Wildflower. Stone.* 2010.
ISBN: 978-1-931247-88-7 (HB) $25

Heinzelman, Kurt. *The Names They Found There.* 2011.
ISBN: 978-1-931247-27-0 $15

LaVilla-Havelin, Jim. *Counting.* 2010.
ISBN: 978-1-931247-80-1 $15

Lyons, Bonnie. *Bedrock.* 2011.
ISBN: 978-1-931247-83-2 $15

Moore, Trey. *Some Will Play the Cello.* 2010.
ISBN: 978-1-931247-70-2 $17

Pettit, Holly. *To One Who Lives on the Mainland.* 2010.
ISBN: 978-1-931247-71-9 $17

Saidi, Mo H. *The Color of Faith.* 2010.
ISBN: 978-1-931247-79-5 $15

Scudder, Emily, *Feeding Time.* 2011.
ISBN: 978-1-931247-91-7 $15

Simon, Beth. *No Mirror, No Hunger.* 2011.
ISBN: 978-1-931247-93-1 $15

Starkey, David. *It Must Be Like the World.* 2011.
ISBN: 978-1-931247084-9 $15

Valdata, Pat. *Inherent Vice.* 2011.
ISBN: 978-1-931247-30-6 $15

Wing, Avra. *Recurring Dream.* 2011.
ISBN: 978-1-931247-92-4 $7

**For a complete listing of Pecan Grove Press titles,
please visit our website at *http://library.stmarytx.edu/pgpress***